Guidelines

Concerning the Academic

MANDATUM

IN CATHOLIC UNIVERSITIES

(CANON 812)

CABRINI COLLEGE LIBRARY
610 King of Prussia Road
Radnor, PA 19087

United States Conference of Catholic Bishops

Washington, D.C.

LC
487
.G85
2001

#47773260

In December 2000 the NCCB Ad Hoc Committee on the *Mandatum* sent a draft copy of these guidelines to all Bishops for their use in conversations on the local level with theologians. The final draft entitled *Guidelines Concerning the Academic* Mandatum *in Catholic Universities* was discussed and accepted for publication by the general membership at its June 2001 General Meeting. The guidelines have been authorized for publication by the undersigned.

Msgr. William P. Fay
General Secretary
USCCB

First Printing, July 2001

ISBN 1-57455-430-1

Copyright © 2001, United States Conference of Catholic Bishops, Inc., Washington, D.C. All rights reserved. No part of this work may be reproduced or transmitted in any form or by any means, electronic or mechanical, including photocopying, recording, or by any information storage and retrieval system, without permission in writing from the copyright holder.

Contents

Preface

O n November 17, 1999, the Catholic Bishops of the United States approved *The Application of Ex corde Ecclesiae for the United States*, implementing the apostolic constitution *Ex corde Ecclesiae*. This action received the *recognitio* from the Congregation for Bishops on May 3, 2000. Bishop Joseph A. Fiorenza, President of the United States Conference of Catholic Bishops (USCCB) (formerly the National Conference of Catholic Bishops [NCCB]), decreed that the *Application* would have the force of particular law for the United States on May 3, 2001.

Guidelines

P ope John Paul II's constitution *Ex corde Ecclesiae* of 1990 fostered a productive dialogue between the Bishops of the United States and the leaders of Catholic colleges and universities. It is anticipated that this recently approved *Application of Ex corde Ecclesiae for the United States* will further that conversation and build a community of trust and dialogue between Bishops and theologians. Without ongoing and respectful communication, the implementation of the *mandatum* might appear to be only a juridical constriction of the work of theologians. Both Bishops and theologians are engaged in a necessary though complementary service to the Church that requires ongoing and mutually respectful dialogue.

Article 4, 4, e, iv, of the *Application* states that "a detailed procedure will be developed outlining the process of requesting and granting (or withdrawing) the *mandatum*." These guidelines are intended to explain and serve as a resource for the conferral of the *mandatum*. Only those guidelines herein that repeat a norm of the *Application* have the force of particular law. They were accepted for distribution to the members of the USCCB on June 15, 2001, by the Conference's general membership.

1. Nature of the *mandatum*

a. The *mandatum* is fundamentally an acknowledgment by church authority that a Catholic professor of a theological discipline is teaching within the full communion of the Catholic Church (*Application*: Article 4, 4, e, i).

b. The object of the *mandatum* is the content of the professor's teaching, and thus the *mandatum* recognizes both the professor's "lawful freedom of inquiry" (*Application*: Article 2, 2) and the professor's commitment and responsibility to teach authentic Catholic doctrine and to refrain from putting forth as Catholic teaching anything contrary to the Church's magisterium (cf. *Application*: Article 4, 4, e, iii).

c. The *mandatum* should not be construed as an appointment, authorization, delegation, or approbation of one's teaching by church authorities. Theologians who have received a *mandatum* are not catechists; they teach in their own name in virtue of their baptism and their academic and professional competence, not in the name of the Bishop or of the Church's magisterium (*Application*: Article 4, 4, e, ii).

2. Who is required to have the *mandatum*?

a. All Catholics who teach theological disciplines in a Catholic university are required to have a *mandatum* (canon 812 and *Application*: Article 4, 4, e).

b. In accord with canon 812, the *mandatum* is an obligation of the professor, not of the university.

c. "Teaching" in this context signifies regular presentation (by full-time or part-time professors) of academic material in an academic institution. Occasional lectures as well as preaching and counseling are not within the meaning of the *Application* and these guidelines.

d. "Theological disciplines" in this context signifies Sacred Scripture, dogmatic theology, moral theology, pastoral theology, canon law, liturgy, and church history (cf. canon 252).

e. "University" in this context signifies not only institutions that bear the title "university" but also Catholic colleges and other institutions of higher learning.

3. Who is to grant the *mandatum*?

a. The *mandatum* is to be granted by the diocesan Bishop of the diocese in which the Catholic university is located, generally understood to be where the president and central administration offices are located (cf. *Application*: Article 4, 4, e , iv, [1]).

b. The competent ecclesiastical authority may grant the *mandatum* personally or through a delegate (*Application*: Article 4, 4, e, iv, [1]).

4. How is the *mandatum* to be granted?

a. A request for a *mandatum* by a professor of a Catholic theological discipline should be in writing and should include a declaration that the teacher will teach in full communion with the Church.

b. The ecclesiastical authority should respond in writing (*Application*: Article 4, 4, e, iv, [3]) (see Appendix for samples).

c. An ecclesiastical authority has the right to offer the *mandatum* on his own initiative (which requires an acceptance), provided that the commitment to teach in full communion with the Church is clear.

d. A professor already hired by the effective date (May 3, 2001) of the *Application* is required to obtain the *mandatum* by June 1, 2002.

   A professor hired after the effective date of the *Application* is required to obtain the *mandatum* within the academic year or within six months of the date of being hired, whichever is longer.

   If the professor does not obtain the *mandatum* within the time period given above, the competent ecclesiastical authority should notify the appropriate authority in the college or university.

e. Without prejudice to the rights of the diocesan Bishop, a *mandatum*, once granted, remains in effect wherever and as long as the professor teaches unless and until it is withdrawn by the competent ecclesiastical authority (*Application*: Article 4, 4, e, iv, [2]). Although there is no need for the *mandatum*, once granted, to be granted again by another diocesan Bishop, every diocesan Bishop has the right to require otherwise in his own diocese (*Application*: footnote 43).

f. If the Bishop is contemplating the denial or withdrawal of the *mandatum*, he should discuss this informally with the theologian, listing the reasons and identifying the sources, and allowing the theologian to make all appropriate responses.

4

5. Grounds and process for withholding or withdrawing the *mandatum*

a. If all the conditions for granting the *mandatum* are fulfilled, the professor has a right to receive it and ecclesiastical authority has an obligation in justice to grant it.

b. Right intentions and right conduct are to be presumed until the contrary is proven. Hence the ecclesiastical authority should presume, until the contrary is proven, that those who attest that they teach in full communion with the Church actually do so.

c. Ecclesiastical authorities who, after discussion with the professor in question, withhold or withdraw the *mandatum* must state their reasons in writing and otherwise enable the person who believes that his or her rights have been violated to seek recourse (*Application*: Article 4, 4, e, [3]; footnote 44). Such withholding or withdrawal should be based on specific and detailed evidence that the teacher does not fulfill the conditions of the *mandatum* (these guidelines: 1, b, and c, supra; *Application*: Article 4, 4, e, iii; NCCB, *Doctrinal Responsibilities: Approaches to Promoting Cooperation and Resolving Misunderstandings Between Bishops and Theologians* [Washington, D.C.: United States Catholic Conference, 1989], III, C, 4).

d. Any negative judgment concerning an objectionable portion of a professor's work should be assessed at three levels: (1) the significance of that portion of the professor's work within the context of his or her overall theological contribution; (2) its relationship to the larger Catholic tradition;

(3) its implications for the life of the Church (cf. *Doctrinal Responsibilities*, III, C, 4).

6. Appeals and resolution of disputes

a. Because the decision to withhold or withdraw the *mandatum* touches on the rights of theologians, the general principles of canon law should be adhered to in seeking recourse and in the process of appeal.

b. In the resolution of disputes about the withholding or withdrawal of the *mandatum*, it is important for both parties to have competent canonical and theological counsel.

c. For the resolution of disputes about the withholding or withdrawal of the *mandatum*, there should be that contact between the Bishop and the professor as urged in canon 1733 § 1. The process set forth in *Doctrinal Responsibilities* should be followed. The right of all parties to good reputation must always be honored (cf. canon 220).

d. Other means for conflict resolution on the diocesan, regional, or provincial levels (not excluding local mediation procedures) can also be invoked (cf. canon 1733).

e. While the use of informal procedures is preferable, the aggrieved party always has the right to formal recourse against the denial or withdrawal of a *mandatum* in accordance with the canonical norms for "Recourse Against Administrative Decrees" (canons 1732-1739).

7. Diocesan Bishops who have Catholic colleges or universities in their dioceses are encouraged to be available to meet with professors of Catholic theological disciplines to review concrete procedures for the granting, withholding, or withdrawal of the *mandatum* and to discuss other matters of common interest.

8. The members of the USCCB Committee for Bishops and Catholic Colleges and University Presidents and its staff will serve as resource personnel for information and guidance on matters connected with the *mandatum*.

9. These guidelines are to be reviewed after five years by a committee appointed by the Conference President.

APPENDIX

Sample *Mandatum* Draft

ATTESTATION OF THE PROFESSOR OF CATHOLIC THEOLOGICAL DISCIPLINES

I hereby declare my role and responsibility as a professor of a Catholic theological discipline within the full communion of the Church.

As a professor of a Catholic theological discipline, therefore, I am committed to teach authentic Catholic doctrine and to refrain from putting forth as Catholic teaching anything contrary to the Church's magisterium.

SIGNATURE: _____

DATE: _____

PLACE: _____

ACKNOWLEDGMENT OF DIOCESAN BISHOP

I hereby acknowledge your declaration to remain within the full communion of the Catholic Church in fulfillment of your role and responsibility as a professor of Catholic theological disciplines.

I recognize your commitment as a professor of Catholic theological disciplines to teach authentic Catholic doctrine and to refrain from putting forth as Catholic teaching anything contrary to the Church's magisterium.

While the *mandatum* does not constitute you as an agent of the magisterium, it does affirm that your work as a professor of Catholic theological disciplines is an important part of the Church's mission.

This *mandatum* remains in effect as long as you are engaged in the teaching of theology or until it is withdrawn by competent ecclesiastical authority for a just cause.

SIGNATURE: _____

DATE: _____

PLACE: _____

Sample *Mandatum* Draft Offered by the Bishop on his own Initiative

MEMORANDUM

TO: Professor Thomas Bellarmine

FROM: Most Reverend Angelo Buonpastore

RE: *MANDATUM*

DATE:

This memorandum constitutes the *mandatum* that you are required to have in order to be in compliance with canon 812. The purpose of the *mandatum* is to recognize the mutual ecclesial relationship that exists between the Church and Catholic professors of theology. It also constitutes my grateful response to your participation in the Church's mission.

I hereby acknowledge your role and responsibility as a professor of Catholic theology within the full communion of the Catholic Church.

As a professor of Catholic theology you are committed to teach authentic Catholic doctrine and to refrain from putting forth as Catholic teaching anything contrary to the Church's magisterium.

While this *mandatum* does not constitute you as an agent of the magisterium, it does affirm that your work as a professor of theology is an important part of the Church's mission.

This *mandatum* remains in effect as long as you are engaged in the teaching of Catholic theology or until it is withdrawn by appropriate authority for a just cause.

This *mandatum* takes effect upon my receipt of the enclosed statement of your understanding and acceptance of its terms.

ACKNOWLEDGMENT

I, **Thomas Bellarmine**, have reviewed the *mandatum* conferred on me by Bishop Angelo Buonpastore and, by means of my signature, express my understanding and acceptance of its terms.

SIGNATURE: _____

DATE: _____

PLACE: _____

RESOURCE COMPANION

This protocol was developed by USCCB staff in consultation with the Ad Hoc Committee on the Mandatum *to assist Diocesan Bishops, Catholic professors of Catholic theological disciplines, and presidents of Catholic colleges and universities in the implementation of the* Guidelines Concerning the Academic *Mandatum* in Catholic Universities. *This protocol was not subject to a vote by the Bishops.*

Professors of Catholic Theological Disciplines and the *Mandatum*

1. Catholic professor of Catholic theological disciplines requests a *mandatum*

a. The Catholic professor of Catholic theological disciplines writes to the Bishop of the diocese where the university is located (if there are branches, the diocese where the central administrative offices are located) requesting the *mandatum* and stating that s/he will teach in communion with the Church.

b. When the professor receives notification that the *mandatum* has been granted, s/he may wish to inform the chair of the Theology Department and/or the president of the university.

c. If the professor is notified that conditions for granting the *mandatum* may not be fulfilled for reasons given in writing, the professor should

(1) meet with the Bishop, if s/he has not already done so, to discuss the action, the evidence, and the reasons for the Bishop's decision, and/or

(2) be accompanied by theological and canonical counsel when meeting with the Bishop.

d. Following the meeting, the Bishop

(1) notifies the professor in writing and grants the *mandatum*, or

(2) notifies the professor in writing that he will not grant the *mandatum* giving his reasons in the written notification.

e. If the professor does not receive the *mandatum*, and s/he believes his or her rights have been violated, the professor has a right to

(1) seek resolution through the formal process described in *Doctrinal Responsibilities*,

(2) seek resolution through other means for conflict resolution that exist in the diocese, and/or

(3) seek formal recourse in accord with canons 1732-1739, "Recourse Against Administrative Decrees."

f. If the professor decides to seek resolution of the dispute, s/he should obtain theological and canonical counsel throughout the process.

g. If the professor decides to seek resolution of the dispute, the Bishop should participate in the process, whether the process is informal or formal.

h. The Bishop notifies the president of the college/university of the granting/denial of the *mandatum* to the professor(s) of theological disciplines.

i. Public acknowledgment of the granting, refusal by the Bishop or the professor, withdrawing of the *mandatum* for professors of Catholic theological disciplines, and responses to inquiries regarding these matters should be made in accord with a procedure worked out, with appropriate counsel, by the Bishop and college/university presidents within a diocese.

2. Catholic professor of Catholic theological disciplines receives a *mandatum* from the Bishop offered on his own initiative

a. The *mandatum* is offered in writing at the initiative of the diocesan Bishop. A professor receives a *mandatum* from the Bishop of the diocese in which the college/university where s/he teaches is located. The professor is asked to respond within a specified time period indicating his or her commitment to teach in communion with the Church.

b. The professor accepts the *mandatum*,

   (1) acknowledges the *mandatum* in writing stating that s/he will teach in communion with the Church, and
   (2) may wish to inform the president of the college/university.

c. If the professor does not wish to accept the *mandatum*, s/he

   (1) notifies the Bishop in writing of the decision giving reasons for the non-acceptance, and
   (2) may wish to inform the president of the college/university.

d. The Bishop notifies the president of the college/university of the acceptance/non-acceptance of the *mandatum* by the professor(s) of Catholic theological disciplines.

e. If a professor chooses not to respond to the Bishop regarding acceptance or non-acceptance of the *mandatum* within the specified time period, the Bishop may wish to notify the president of the college/university of the non-response.

f. Public acknowledgment of the granting, refusal by the Bishop or the professor, withdrawing of the *mandatum* for professors of Catholic theological disciplines, and responses to inquiries regarding these matters should be made in accord with a procedure worked out, with appropriate counsel, by the Bishop and college/university presidents within a diocese.

Diocesan Bishop and the *Mandatum*

1. Diocesan Bishop grants *mandatum* upon request from Catholic professor of Catholic theological disciplines

a. The diocesan Bishop determines whether he will delegate the authority to grant the *mandatum* and, if so, to whom.

b. The diocesan Bishop receives a request from a Catholic professor teaching a Catholic theological discipline in a Catholic college or university in his diocese for a *mandatum*.

(1) If he has delegated the authority to grant the *mandatum*, he forwards the request to the delegate.

(2) If he has reserved the authority to grant the *mandatum* to himself, he reviews the request to confirm that the professor

    i. is teaching a Catholic theological discipline, and

    ii. has stated that s/he will teach in communion with the Church.

(3) If the professor of Catholic theological disciplines teaches in a branch of the college/university located in another diocese, the Bishop may wish to consult the diocesan Bishop of the diocese in which the branch is located regarding the conditions for granting the *mandatum*.

c. If the conditions for granting the *mandatum* are fulfilled in the request,

(1) the Bishop grants the *mandatum*, and

(2) notifies the president of the college/university.

d. Public acknowledgment of the granting, refusal by the Bishop or the professor, withdrawing of the *mandatum* for professors of Catholic theological disciplines, and responses to inquiries regarding these matters should be made in accord with a procedure worked out, with appropriate counsel, by the Bishop and college/university presidents within a diocese.

2. Diocesan Bishop offers *mandatum* to Catholic professor of Catholic theological disciplines on his own initiative

a.   The diocesan Bishop requests names of Catholic professors of Catholic theological disciplines teaching in Catholic colleges and universities in his diocese from the appropriate representatives of the respective institutions.

b.   The diocesan Bishop determines whether he will delegate the authority to grant the *mandatum* and, if so, to whom.

c.   The diocesan Bishop (or his delegate) sends a letter to each professor of Catholic theological disciplines teaching in Catholic colleges and universities in his diocese

   (1) offering the *mandatum,* and
   (2) requesting a response from the professor within a specified time period indicating the professor's commitment to teach in communion with the Church.

d.   The Bishop receives

   (1) response of acceptance from professor,

   i.   acknowledges the response, and
   ii. notifies the president of the college/university.

   (2) response of non-acceptance from professor,

   i.   acknowledges the response, and
   ii. notifies the president of the college/university.

(3) no response from professor after specified time period has lapsed and so may wish to notify the president of the college/university of the non-response.

e. Public acknowledgment of the granting, refusal by the Bishop or the professor, withdrawing of the *mandatum* for professors of Catholic theological disciplines, and responses to inquiries regarding these matters should be made in accord with a procedure worked out, with appropriate counsel, by the Bishop and college/university presidents within a diocese.

3. Diocesan Bishop denies *mandatum* for Catholic professor of Catholic theological disciplines

a. The diocesan Bishop determines whether he will delegate the authority to grant the *mandatum* and, if so, to whom.

b. The diocesan Bishop receives a request from a Catholic professor teaching a Catholic theological discipline in a Catholic college or university in his diocese for a *mandatum*.

(1) If he has delegated the authority to grant the *mandatum*, he forwards the request to the delegate.

(2) If he has reserved the authority to grant the *mandatum* to himself, he reviews the request to confirm that the professor

i. is teaching a Catholic theological discipline, and
ii. has stated that s/he will teach in communion with the Church.

(3) If the professor of Catholic theological disciplines teaches in a branch of the college/university located in another diocese, the Bishop may wish to consult the diocesan Bishop of the diocese in which the branch is located regarding the conditions for granting the *mandatum*.

c. If the conditions for granting the *mandatum* are fulfilled in the request,

(1) the Bishop grants the *mandatum*, and
(2) notifies the president of the college/university.

d. If the conditions for granting the *mandatum* do not seem to be fulfilled, the Bishop, if he judges it appropriate, asks theological and canonical counsel to review the evidence and advise him.

e. If, after hearing counsel, the Bishop determines that the conditions for granting the *mandatum* are fulfilled, he responds to the professor in writing and grants the *mandatum*.

f. If, after hearing counsel, the Bishop determines that the conditions for granting the *mandatum* may not be fulfilled,

(1) he notifies the professor in writing, and
(2) requests a meeting with the professor to discuss the evidence, stating that s/he may be accompanied by theological and canonical counsel.

g. Following the meeting, the Bishop decides whether or not the conditions for granting the *mandatum* are fulfilled. The Bishop

(1) notifies the professor in writing and grants the *mandatum*, or

(2) notifies the professor in writing that he will not grant the *mandatum* giving his reasons in the written notification, and

(3) notifies the president of the college/university of his decision.

h. If the professor does not receive the *mandatum*, and s/he believes his or her rights have been violated, the professor has a right to

(1) seek resolution through the formal process described in *Doctrinal Responsibilities*,

(2) seek resolution through other means for conflict resolution that exist in the diocese, and/or

(3) seek formal recourse in accord with canons 1732-1739, "Recourse Against Administrative Decrees."

i. If the professor decides to seek resolution of the dispute, the Bishop should participate in the process, whether the process is informal or formal.

j. Public acknowledgment of the granting, refusal by the Bishop or the professor, withdrawing of the *mandatum* for professors of Catholic theological disciplines, and responses to inquiries regarding these matters should be made in accord with a procedure worked out, with appropriate counsel, by the Bishop and college/university presidents within a diocese.

4. Diocesan Bishop withdraws *mandatum* from Catholic professor of Catholic theological disciplines

a. The diocesan Bishop is informed in writing that a Catholic professor of Catholic theological disciplines who possesses a *mandatum* is not fulfilling the condition of the *mandatum*, that is, the Catholic professor is alleged not to be teaching in communion with the Church or to be teaching contrary to the Church's magisterium. The allegation must be written, specific as to a particular writing or public lecture, and it must detail on what grounds the teaching is not in conformity with the magisterium.

b. The diocesan Bishop

   (1) reviews the allegation and the evidence,
   (2) seeks theological and canonical counsel,
   (3) consults other appropriate individuals, and
   (4) determines whether or not the allegation is reasonable and the evidence sufficient to support the allegation.

c. If the diocesan Bishop determines that the grounds for the allegation are neither reasonable nor sufficient, he communicates this to the one(s) making the allegation.

d. If the diocesan Bishop determines the allegation is reasonable and the evidence sufficient to support the allegation, he

   (1) notifies the professor of the allegation(s) and the source of the allegation(s) in writing, and
   (2) requests a meeting with the professor to discuss the evidence, stating that s/he may be accompanied by theological and canonical counsel.

e. During the meeting with the professor, the diocesan Bishop, accompanied by theological and canonical counsel,

(1) presents the allegation, identifying its source,
(2) reviews the evidence alleging that the professor has violated the condition of the *mandatum*,
(3) provides opportunity for defense by the professor, and
(4) informs the professor of his or her right to seek recourse in the event that the professor believes his or her rights have been violated.

f. Following the meeting, the diocesan Bishop, after hearing from counsel, decides whether or not he will withdraw the *mandatum*.

(1) If the diocesan Bishop decides not to withdraw the *mandatum*, he

i. notifies the professor of his decision in writing,
ii. notifies the one(s) making the allegation of his decision, and
iii. may wish to notify the president of the college/ university of his decision.

(2) If the diocesan Bishop decides to withdraw the *mandatum*, he

i. notifies the professor in writing that he is withdrawing the *mandatum* giving his reasons,
ii. informs the professor of his or her right to recourse in the event that the professor believes his or her rights have been violated, and
iii. notifies the president of the college/university of his decision.

g. If the diocesan Bishop withdraws the *mandatum*, and the professor believes his or her rights have been violated, the professor has a right to

(1) seek resolution through the formal process described in *Doctrinal Responsibilities,*
(2) seek resolution through other means for conflict resolution that exist in the diocese, and/or
(3) seek formal recourse in accord with canons 1732-1739, "Recourse Against Administrative Decrees."

h. If the professor decides to seek resolution of the dispute, the diocesan Bishop should participate in the process, whether the process is informal or formal.

i. Public acknowledgment of the granting, refusal by the Bishop or the professor, withdrawing of the *mandatum* for professors of Catholic theological disciplines, and responses to inquiries regarding these matters should be made in accord with a procedure worked out, with appropriate counsel, by the Bishop and college/university presidents within a diocese.

President of Catholic College/ University and the *Mandatum*

A. Upon request of the diocesan Bishop or his delegate, the president or the appropriate representative of the Catholic college/ university forwards a list of Catholic professors of Catholic theological disciplines teaching in the college/university.

B. Following notification of the president by the diocesan Bishop or his delegate of the names of Catholic professors of Catholic theological disciplines in the college/university who have received, been denied, or explicitly or implicitly not accepted the *mandatum*, the president may wish to inform appropriate college/university personnel in accord with college/university policy.

C. Public acknowledgment of the granting, refusal by the Bishop or the professor, withdrawing of the *mandatum* for Catholic professors of theological disciplines, and responses to inquiries regarding these matters should be made in accord with a procedure worked out, with appropriate counsel, by the Bishop and college/university presidents within a diocese.

(1) Possible points to consider in developing a procedure:

i. The *mandatum* is an acknowledgment by church authority that the professor teaches in communion with the Church.

ii. The acknowledgment takes place in the external forum.

iii. Neither the Bishop nor the college/university is obliged to publish a list of professors who have received *mandata*, though either may wish to do so after appropriate consultation.

iv. In the absence of a published list, and when asked about a particular professor and the *mandatum*, the president might

1. respond affirmatively or negatively without details,

2. refer the inquiry to the Bishop, or

3. respond in accord with a procedure determined in consultation with the diocesan Bishop and other appropriate persons.

e. Reasons why a particular professor does not have a *mandatum* should not be made public without prior knowledge of the professor.

(2) The procedure should be communicated to professors of Catholic theological disciplines.

10314BC 311
LBC
12-18-01 30368   FM